Dreaming
Outside
of
Destiny

Roberto Carlos Martinez

PublishAmerica
Baltimore

ISBN: 1-60703-781-5
PUBLISHED BY PUBLISHAMERICA, LLLP
www.publishamerica.com
Baltimore

Printed in the United States of America

For my brother Walter,

We have so much to learn from life and from each other. Let us make the best of time, for nothing is certain but the breathing moments.

Introduction (For the Soul)

For the Soul I

The lies may fade away,
like the one who used them.
But the truth,
the truth will be here.
It will be eternal like the one who spoke of it.

He who spoke the truth,
will bathe in clean waters,
the clean water will see no
dirt or soil,
for his soul had always been cleansed.

For the Soul II

When they stop hearing me,
when they stop hearing me,
when I stop hearing me,
I will still hear him.

Deep inside of me,
like the water, the bread, that
keeps this physical body alive.

I will hear him,
and in him I will hear myself,
for I was never too far away from him.

For the Soul III

I will not ask for destruction,
I will not ask for destruction on them.
They may receive no pain or pleasure.

All I ask is for peace,
for my own peace,
and let them find peace in what they have
created.

Let them find peace,
but not the pain for others.

For the Soul IV

A grave will be the resting place for my flesh.
A sky will be the resting place for my soul.
Where I will no longer dream of what was meant to be.
Never cry for what I thought I deserved.

The Strongest Love

The strongest love is the one we destroy and is reborn once more.

The one we drown and slowly rises out of the sea.

It forgives, loves you for everything you are.

It smiles in the dark,
captures moonlight and reflects sunlight.

It swims in freedom and dances in truth,
looking at you firmly in the eyes.

It needs no ground, for there is no surface
that can contain it.

Dreamer

I acquired a taste of her,
the beautiful woman of my dreams,
stole a piece of my excited heart
under the moonlight.

Playfully intelligent,
seductive goddess with beautiful dazzling blue eyes
and gripping Cleopatra lips.
I surrender to her once again,
she has haunted me in my dreams,
made me an insomniac but at the same time a dreamer.

A Thousand Times

A thousand times I heard you whispering my name,
in the early morning
on the bed where we once made love.
I would lay there, still, cold stone of earth.

I was a man, I was man,

For my selfish ego cowered into my brain and,
would not let me go,
would not let me go to you.

Perhaps I was a foolish man.
No matter how much I loved you,
I would sit there and wait,
on top of the whiteness of the sheets,
in the dreamlike white of the room.

Flesh

Flesh, physical thing holding me captive.
In the green grass,
in the green grass it used to role.

Flesh, physical thing holding me captive.
The soul dances, but at times it does not move.

Rotten stench it has begun to acquire.

In the burning fire, in the burning fire.
Many think it will burn.

But I become dust at the site of death,
I become the one who cared.

Dust, dust.
Lovely particles that shall be of my flesh.

This

I am overwhelmed in the despair I produced inside my mind.
I watch, I watch this dark sky that hovers over me.

This, this thing that desperately holds me prisoner inside of
me.

Forgive this sinner.
Forgive this flesh.
That hungers for more.

Breakout

The feeling thrusts itself into me,
an unforgiving sadness of life embraces me.

I begin to over think it.
I hope this is hell and when we die we are going to heaven.

I must have. I must have done something really bad to
deserve this.
In a past life, what did I do?

"Come to bed," says my body lying on the bed as my spirit
sits in a corner of the room.

Traitor

I crawl through the sun dried grass making my way to what
they said was there.
I find nothing.
Lonely, stupid, fake words they had used.

Anger takes over,
the bright red color of the inside of a broken watermelon.
Juicy red, wet, empty and full at the same time.

Traitor, Traitor.
You did it again.
Played this game with me.
Played with this fire.

Better than This

I never was better than this.
Dried, brown, rusted looking lettuce I became.
I took the shape of an autumn leaf to distract you.

Foolish being, I never was better than this,
because of you, I learned to regenerate my soul.

I take the distinct smell of green peppers in the hot sun,
the beautiful color of a fried plantain.

I never was better than this,
carefully destructive in what I choose to be.

Fresh

Fresh,
perfect in my fat banana shape.

Fresh.
Did you feel the smell of my desire?
Crazy, beautiful, opened lust.

I taste from the beautiful flower.

Stones

They do not wonder,
useless stones,
useless stones,
they do not wonder.

They go nowhere.
No voice, no movement.
A breath trapped in time.

Useless stones,
useless stones.

Voiceless significance trapped in a napkin jar.

Always Wanted

I've always wanted to love like in the movies.
Not like in the naughty ones, but like in the romantic ones.

We are all different,
some gently tender,
some wildly spicy.

I've always wanted to love like in the movies.
Not like in the naughty ones, but like in the romantic ones.

I've always wanted to trust,
to feel like nothing matters in that moment,
to feel that nothing matters because it's that good.

Land of Dreams

We considered everything we had done; crossed the border humanity had built, made some kids, and purchased a home.

Memories guided us through all the things we once dreamt of.

Soon, we would meet our dream destroyer, the one who "caught" our dreams in a gold web, devouring them like cotton candy.

These Eyes

Take these eyes that no longer see the world as bright as in
my childhood,
take these hands that dangle like suicidal ropes,
and these feet that no longer desire to be placed on the
ground.

Don't forget this brain that has failed to function ever since
it stopped thinking for itself.

It Was Written

Your fate was clearly written in the palm of your hand.

Fool, you must cover your mouth, for you start to stutter
when you lie.

How sure you are of your lies, only you know.
Squared lips fail to say truth in your cylindrical shape of
cowering defeat.
What the world sees, you must have lost it in a head screw.

Once Again

In the darkness of my thoughts, I feel your kiss on my lips.
Traitor type of heart, loving type of voice.
I let you in to tear me apart,
making me feel human once again.

Helped

Foolish it is, to think we are stronger than love,
or perhaps we think we are stronger than our need to be
helped.

I Am Not Broken

They love me more than I love myself.

They themselves are lost,
but they've found a way to take it.

Everyday I awaken.
With a ruptured dream of how things could be.

I am not broken.
I am not broken.

Many times I tied myself to the mirror,
to see who I really was or wanted to be.

Sometimes I start to bleed,
but I find the way,
I find the way to heal myself,
I use the cobwebs to heal my wounds.

I am still here.

It's this physical thing that holds me here.

My temple.

Lingering

I feel suppression in my soul.
I am lingering at the top of an hour-glass
like the last particle of sand,
trying to defy this, this emotion, this destiny.

In Her

She stopped breathing a long time ago,
the one who used to whisper to me in the corner of the
room.
She stopped breathing a long time ago.
The death, I had longed smelled in her.

We Got Here

Putrid smell of fear,
my senses that smell did take.
A child hiding under the bed,
because the unmindful war could take lives.

So young I learned the stench of death.
The bodies, burning in the hot sun,
because there wasn't enough time to bury them.
Was it death or assassination?

War.
War.
Agony in the word itself.

Many lands we crossed to come here,
many tears we cried to get here.

We got here.

We got here.

So did the war.

Falling

Passionate love transformed into emotional obsession.
Extreme surrender to who I am.

Falling…

Come to me rebirth, new origin.

A delicate love you dragged from deep inside me.

Human Heart

If understanding leads to truth,
then truth leads to heaven.

What we don't understand aggravates us,
we let that negative energy take us over.

We forget to understand,
to look with our hearts,
with our human heart.

Days

There are days when we awake angry,
possibly the reflection of a dream or a change in the weather.

Energies

At the end of the day,
the body has collected so much,
this temple that captures energy, captures love.

At the end of the day,
we must listen to it,
love it and help it relax.

A bit of meditation,
to let go of those energies that others have clung to you.

Stop

Sometimes I get a feeling that one day it's all going to stop.
A dream fading away like a lemon in a waste disposal.

I'll leave a fresh smell.
A memory trapped in time.

They may remember me, those who will stay.

Weakness

"I didn't make you do it," says the perpetrator.
True, you did not,
but slowly you crept into my mind.
Filled me with words and played with my heart.

When you take over,
my mind is the instrument you play.
You do not use your hands,
but you use words and the weakness of a mind.

My Last Moments

During my last moments,
You take me back to the blue sea,
to the fertile earth with the fruitful trees.

You take me back to the beginning of the wind's whisper,
to the light that once beautified my skin.

During my last moments,
I hear your words,
I feel the warmth in my soul,
and the peace taking me over.

From Ourselves

We run,
we run, until there is no where else to go.
Until the light has failed to filter into our brains.

We run,
we run, trying to find that purpose,
that thing that makes us happy.

The happiness is in the struggle.

If we run, we only run from ourselves.

The White Rabbit

My thoughts stumble into a lonely forest of dry trees,
sheltered in green grass.

I find myself chasing the white rabbit,
over and over again,
running after it,
trying to match its skipping speed.

I grab it with my hands,
feeling its breath, the vibration of its heartbeat camouflaged
by its white fur.

I desperately chase after it,
I urgently chase after it.

The Truth

The truth is in you,
the truth is in you,
but you must accept it.

Don't deny what others have, for so long,
the truth,
don't let it break loose.

The truth,
the reason why so many decide to hurt others.
For their truth, they have denied,
negativity and ego has taken over.

What awaits for them their last day, they'll know.

Recover

I wonder if many ever felt like this,
I wonder if they really felt like this from the bottom of their
heart.

Rock, lost in the ocean,
 drop of water, held by the wind over the fire.
Leaf, trapped in the wind, failing to land,
piece of soil set to dry.

If they have, do they deny the feeling or do they live with it?

Perhaps they learn to live with it and one day someone
comes along to erase that feeling.
Sometimes someone has stolen something important to us
and someone else recovers it.

Yours

I gave the scent of my love to you,
and you took it, made it yours.

It Fails

With her, with her I try.
I close my eyes and I try to imagine it is you,
but it fails.

I know you are somewhere far away,
where I am a vanished memory for you.

Seas away, I may never see you again.

I wonder if you think of me.
If I ever fly through your thoughts and if I do, do I ever land?

Broken Promises

They will not discourage me,
of this feeling, of this dream that keeps me up on those
lonely nights.

That dream that turns my nightmares into what they will
never be.

Broken promises,
they will not discourage me,
for they are there to test me.

Barriers that are meant to fall when I am me.

Never Enters

I waited for you,
I waited for you for so long in this dark and empty room,
which has filled itself to the brim with thoughts of your
loneliness.

The coldness of itself has destroyed any warmth of your
presence.

But you never came, I do not understand.

I am a shadow in the dark,
You are the light that never enters.

Reach

Adversity, it has been there for long.
There to inspire me, I don't let it defeat me.

It wraps its thousand arms around me, becoming a prison.
Holding me tightly, I still see what is meant for me.

I go against it.
If I am not blinded, I can still reach it.

Land

A dust particle floats in the air,
sticking to what it touches.

Light as air it becomes,
then it lands.

Sometimes we land.

Possess

You cannot possess me,
I am free,
I was released into a world that craved my existence.

I am part of that world, it could not posses me,
for I am it and it is me.

I learned to walk and I learned to live with those around me.
Later I learned I possessed what many could not.
For there was wisdom, there was greater power.

They thought they could possess that too.

Days Are Splendid

On a splendid day I thank for what I have.

Sometimes that day turns sour,
someone is trying to take me down.

I fight that achy feeling.

The Times

I searched for you in the hidden place of my treasured emotions.

Where you had once laid me to rest for I was seeking no longer.

I lost, I lost you.

I search again,
I search again, not the way I did before.

This time I am stronger and wiser than in the times of my immaturities.

The Physical

The physical still haunts me.
Love, we used to search for each other.
When we found each other, we enjoyed those moments,
seconds trapped
in a sandglass.

I left you, I had to grow,
far away from you.

The physical still haunts me.
In its resplendent beauty, I feel the sensation through my
body.
I feel your lips on mine; soft concentrated sensory particles.

Freed

I freed myself from the illusion that had held me tightly for so long.
Those long lies that had wrapped themselves around me creating a
cocoon from which I could not find an exit.

The lips that had once kissed only one but eventually lost count,
don't know why I let that enchantment hold me prisoner for so long.

That impression that you created in me,
it slithered its way into my heart,
changed its color layer by layer and tore the
wisdom in me.

Falling into deception is not to be permanently lost.

I came back.

I found my way back to who I was.

Predetermined

Predetermined for me, you could not be.
Irresistible, you were, but not determined.
Perhaps it was inevitable for me to fall for you.

The whole time I felt I was under control.
Soon you set your inner self free, inside of me.

You established yourself in me.

I violently tore you out of my heart like tearing moss
off a tree.

A Long Time Ago

The dark brown earth we had once felt in our hands.
It's soft but rough texture, meeting with that of our own.

The seas had once protected us,
we had once heard the waves slamming against the
sunbathed rocks,
and had heard that sound carried by the wind.
The trees had once surrounded us in their sunlit haven.

The seas had protected us,
from what was coming, from a far away place.

A voyage, gone a different direction.

One day it would all change.
In books, we became "ignorant" and "savages."

Lost

Lost, those moments feel.
Running through the open fields,
hidden under the tall grass,
laughing and rolling to its windy vibrations.

Lying there in green,
looking up at the bright sun,
the smell of earth seeping through the warm air.

The sound of the hummingbirds with their wings flapping
and
the bees, hidden under the summer flowers.
The sound of the sea trapped in an old conch shell.

A secret we try to keep from others,
only to later realize it was never trapped there.

Chased

I've chased a dream as it runs like the light of dawn through
a deep forest.
I've held onto it, before it gets close to the cliff.
I hold onto it so hard that it shatters,
leaving me empty handed.

Floating

I set my eyes on your floating memory approaching the sand,
I try to run, but you creep through the sand like a thirsty
desert beast.

Return

The childhood memories,
they run violently through me,
trap me in their despair.

They do not drift,
they do not drift.

They return to shore like fresh dead bodies.

I try to clamp them shut.

Brown-Colored Princess

Brown colored princess.
I've seen you walking through the night with your long black
curly hair
and those wondrous brown eyes.
Far away, you stand from the world that needs you.

There is no hiding under the moonlight.

Brown colored princess, sorry for what he did.

Walk no longer under that darkness.
Walk no longer under that darkness.
Today is a new day, leave that road of despair.

Today is a new day,
let go of the sadness.

Brown colored princess, sorry for what he did to you.

That sinful man that walked through the light,
took everything that he could take from you.

That man who took your "hope diamond" and threw it
ashore.

He left you bare, in that empty space of sadness
from which a smile has not surfaced.

Today is a new day.
Keep dreaming, for time is ticking, and the past is no longer.

Don't drown in the past, swim towards the future.

Physical Thing

Love was never a physical thing,
it has always been of the spirit.

Those who find true love,
never question it.

It goes by a name, a word,
it can go unspoken but seen.

Love was never a physical thing,
it has always been of the spirit.

Though many may call something "love,"
remember that love is not obsessive nor possessive.

Different Now

The broken promises,
the hateful lies,
the torturing sadness,
it does not matter today.

For time ticks away to the rhythm of blood
dripping from a shattered heart.

Don't spend the years thinking of what you could have done,
even chairs grow dusty.
Spend them doing what you want to do,
don't let the years rust away.

It's not over, not today, not this moment.

Against You

The damage this type of life has done,
not just on the exterior, but also the exterior.
Trying to clean what was been destroyed, impossible.

Moving on, an exception to the rule.

Instilling hatred and lies to an offspring, unforgivable.
Only you can forgive yourself.

When you are aching from what came back to you,
that offspring that you sinned against,
will one day use that sin against you.

Book of Sand

Conscious to what I had once experienced.
I leaped into that emotion that had once taken over,
finding you sitting on the edge of that same river.

You looked up at me, from that same book of sand.
You tried, you tried to learn what many have tried to learn
for so long.

I had given up on it already.
My book of sands had been taken by the wind.

I Named You

In my head, I named you.
I named you after that love that had once shook my heart in
a dying sunrise.

You awoke the dream I hid.

You could not replace her.
You can fill a cup with juice instead of water,
but when you crave water nothing else will do.

Sliding on a Tear

The affection I have for you adheres to the walls of my inner
self,
it perpetuates the loss of you.

Then it slides down the wall like a melting piece
of ice sliding on the tear of a broken heart.

Finding that which holds truth,
and that which knows no roof,
of an extent to be what was never meant to be.

From the Altar

Back, to what has stained the path of life.
one who never knew how to love,
he's kin.

It all goes back to that one who was supposed to teach me
how to love,
instead I felt he turned his back to me.

Man!
Many times you did.

I hid behind you,
your big round eyes always gazing straight ahead.

You!
That dark and cold marble statue,
heavy thing that could barely move but had such power.

I stood behind you, where you could not see me.

Waiting and waiting.

With time, every part of you crumbled to pieces before my eyes.

Layer after layer of rock shredded from you.

After the loud roar of crumbling rock,

I heard the loud bang of your big heavy head hit the cement floor,

shattered like glass.

I stood behind you, where you could not see me.

I began to crack too,

layer by layer piece by piece,

in me was a harder interior layer.

Somehow I walked,

to replace you,

a more human thing that could smile without anger,

and could see without jealousy.

I bet the one after me will wait too, but he will never be behind me.

Angel

You descended from heaven with the sound of a swarm of doves in flight,
awoke from your deep sleep with the elegance of a koala bear,
and opened your eyes with the mystique of a black leopard.

From the first time I held you in my arms,
I knew you were special like clear water running down a forest river.

I looked into your big round eyes and saw the miracle of life.
I saw hope like light that shines every corner of a room.
I realized the beginning is never the end and that joy is a continuous cycle.

I felt you grasp my hand,
I had never felt such strength and excitement to live.
I held you close to my ear like a seashell, waiting for the sound of the waves.

I heard love.

From that moment I knew I could never let you go.

But if one day I had to, I knew life would never be the same.

Close to Her

I held her close enough to feel my sadness.
For a second, I thought I heard her heart scream.

I held her and I bet she could feel my love too.

I held her close enough to feel her lips next to mine,
I felt the repetitive rhythm of her soft breath.
For a second, I could hear it, a caress with the sound of a
flute.

I held her and from that moment I could not let go.

Caged

I can't look because it's taking me back into that feeling of
what I cannot change.
I dream, I dream, that I am coming out of the iron cage.

The wind running through the pores on my skin and the
sunlight reflected on my skin.
When I open my eyes, it is what I cannot change.

I see the trees as I look out,
my heart shakes violently from the fear of what is not meant
to be.

Sins

My silence is a reflex to the things they do,
tearing the pieces, tearing the minutes and the hours.

What consists of the pleasurable experience,
finding death in itself,
in a moment,
trapped forever in time like a deadly sin,
possibly the mark of death.

The sky torn in two, families divided, love obstructed.

Selfishness spreading to those who are still searching.
No honesty where there was once love.

Destroying others because someone destroyed you,
must be like carrying the sins of the dead.

The Torment

Erase yourself.
Erase your self from my memory.
I no longer matter to you,
you no longer matter to me.

You play in my dreams,
skipping through every breath,
laughing through every lonely sorrow.

Let me sleep,
let me rest.

Erase yourself from my memory,
so that I no longer feel bad for myself because I loved you.

Dependence

We depend on the kindness of others,
a source of stability and togetherness.

Let us not get halfway through our lives
and destroy that kindness.

Let us give kindness so we may receive it.
give kindness without expecting it.
If we deprive ourselves of that,
we may get to old age and end up lonely.

We Fill the Void

Patience and tolerance,
it all began from the moment we left the womb.
If not taught by our parents,
it was harder to learn.

Patience and tolerance,
why is it that when we lack it,
we fill its void with hatred.

You Can Feel It

Who could tell you how to feel when you were the only one
who felt it at the time.
They could relate, but they could not feel what you feel.

It's all connected,
the interior and the exterior.

A pile of dusty webs and a beautiful garden in one.
Each with its own distinct features,
different shades of green,
wild flowers,
colorful fruits or vegetables.

Each one can feel the destruction,
but it all depends on what you destroy.

Back to Me

She swims back to me,
in my dreams, she swims back to me,
arrives from the sea in a chariot of seaweeds
and a crown of seashells.

Monad

Brightness and darkness must have melted onto me one day.
If you saw the inner me, painted in half white light and have dark night.
One side shines like the stars, the other captivates like night.

Tendencies

She had a tendency of whispering into my ear how much she
loved me
like a butterfly whispers to a hummingbird in flight.
She also had a tendency to start screaming when I wasn't
obedient
like an owner screams at a pet.

Obedience,
I wonder if it is obedience, or submission.
Maybe it is giving into someone you love.
If it is love, I wonder why giving in hurts.

Core

They drained a river dry searching for me.

For the dimness in my brown eyes,
the brown in my rusted skin
and the ugliness in my aged hair.

They could hear,
from under the water,
they could hear the beating of my dying heart.

If only they could hear theirs too.

Monster

Monster.
Destiny.

I bleed red rivers from you and you bleed from me.

You drag me back in,
you drag me back in with the sound of the rustling of tree
branches in a deep forest.
I crawl and I crawl with my bloody fingers and nails.

You pull me in.

You are eternal, but not I.

Kitty

It's cuteness never captured my attention.
I liked it, I must admit,
but it was never a favorite of mine.

I remember that day clearly.
It ran across the dirt floor with a distinct sound of dreaded
death.

It stopped midway,
a woman grabbed a wooden broom and cornered it.

The man walked in,
picked it up and said "where is the cat."

The man grabbed the defenseless but unattractive
creature by its tail and carried it outside of the bedroom.

He placed it in front of the cat,

the cat lounged towards it as if he had not eaten in weeks.
The pounding lead to piece by piece, layer by layer
of blood, flesh, and guts.

In seconds, there was nothing left.
"He must have been hungry," I thought.

The Penalty

Seductress you caused a sweet obsession in me,
playing that game I decided to play.

I had to,
I had to.

I carved a wooden box,
made a smiley face on the front,
picked up her gentle blue eyes from the grass and locked
them in.

Her hair was the color of a romantic sunset,
I threw that down the river,
it was dirty.

I saw her lips,
but I didn't want to kiss them because I did now know where
they had been.

A Failed Dream

A failed dream of love would hide in a repressed memory.

But it would awaken,
to fulfill what it was meant to fulfill.

Many Years

I hid myself under a body of water,
enclosed myself between reality and a dream.

A thousand years of sleep could not remove the feeling,
of what has hid inside of me for so long,
destiny.

Dreams of Love

In the head of someone who believed in a dream.

Feeling so happy in a captured moment that
felt like the happiest day.

Now, must pretend it never mattered.
Left the second one for that first dream is what hurts the
most.

The second dream, was probably worth it.
In the end, they both fade away the way water fades in a
desert.

You search for the second dream again,
but because of the first one, you can't trust the second one
either.

Steps

You blame yourself the first time,
the second time you blame the world too,
the third time, if you succeed, you learn to value what you
worked so hard for.
For some, it may even take the fourth, fifth, or even the tenth
time.

They will treasure it even more.

Much

The flower never laughed when it was crushed by a human foot,
Nor did it smile or have the chance to take another breath,
and the tree never enjoyed as the tree cutter took its life away.

Humans never laughed as their bones crashed on a concrete floor,
after falling from the height of a five story building.
There wasn't another breath, but a sigh of relief if death had carried the soul away.

What is an end with no beginning,
what is a beginning with no end,
but crumbs of a story left untold.

The Friendliness

Screams were never meant to be friendly.
They were meant to annoy, demand respect,
or hurt the feelings of those who cared.

Once in our childhood,
maybe we screamed at some how much we loved them.
Then, a scream meant something.
A scream coming from our hearts,
the feeling of what we thought would last forever.

Now, we scream over the unhappiness that will not go away.

The Damage

When we get caught in the moment,
we do not think of the damage a lover could do to us,
of the respect we lose for ourselves,
for our temple,
for our soul.

When the illusion ends,
we are left with the beads of reality like a rosary that is torn
into pieces.

In Our Younger Days

Those days,
it was not who we loved that mattered,
but how we loved them.

How we created our own web of desire,
putting every piece of the dream together.

Those days,
it was not who we loved that mattered,
but how we loved them.

We tied ourselves together,
we tied ourselves together because one thought it would last
forever.

Only one knew the exit,
the other one,
was left trapped in the web that had once meant something.

Grasp

You're a stranger to me after so many years,
uninvited rock in an ocean of despair.

It's what humans do.
We find our way,
We find a way away,
away from our own connection of the soul.

Perhaps we broke what was sacred,
Or we forgot to say "I am sorry."

We let it go.

"We let it go" in our own way,
but what was not said caused something to
grasp, to grasp tightly to a soul,
never letting go.

Discovering

You're words floated down the entrance to my
soul like a ball of light floats through the African savannah.

You discovered the weakness in me the way discoverers
discover what has already existed.

You, you discovered I was human under this empty egg
shell.

Resistance

Still here,
trapped in the memories that encaged themselves in my
head.

In every breath and every thought,
I see you.

Your mind, it is resting,
mine, it's still digesting what you left here.

It cannot resist the notion of this love.
An emotion awakening the sleeper in his dream that
disillusions.

Essence

Before my eyes begin to fail,
let me see you once again,
in the perfection of your undisrupted physical self.

Stay with me,
in the last minutes before my departure,
never letting go.
Hold onto the seconds,
to the rhythm of my breath,
and fading of my heartbeat.

Today will fade,
so will tomorrow.
The essence, it will still remember you.

Dummy

I force myself,
I force myself,
through the stone walls of this unforgettable feeling.

White, it does, it does become all.

My conscious,
it does not rest.

For you are still here somehow,
that loneliness you left,
it speaks to me.

I become something that has life,
but does not move.

Bean

An unstable deliciousness that transcends the test of time
like memories that have clung to rebirth.
A red bean, trapped in a sack of white beans.

It stands out from the rest,
there is no hiding place.

There are times when it loses itself,
but it finds the way out to its own identity.

Free

Be free, free.
For there is no such thing as perfection,
only human labels and standards.

Don't be deceived by what we were never meant to be.
Try your best, but never change for others.
Others may be more lost than you.

What is inside matters most,
for the outside will one day fade away.
Let the exterior be another shell to reflect what is inside.

The Luring

The wasted time,
the wasted lies we both drained from ourselves.
You pretended to be me and I pretended to be you.

You came,
You came to me,
and you submerged the burning flame in me.

Without fire,
I was not me,
Without the smile,
I was not me.

When I awoke from that deep and dark sleep,
I closed the door to everything you had opened in me,
for you could no longer lure me into what I could not be.

The Reason

On a cool early morning,
a small ant manages to hold on to the left foot
of a harpy eagle landing in the dense rainforest.

The bird spreads its wings and begins to fly swiftly through
the trees.

As it begins to rain,
the ant holds on tighter,
noticing the things it had never seen.

It knows that at anytime its legs will let go,
it's body at mercy of the wind.

Above the canopy,
the ant can hold on no longer,
and it leaves the bird's foot,
taking a ride on a falling drop of water.

The ant lands not very far away,
on a tree stump.

Frozen, it gazes at the deforestation where it has landed.
Trapped, like a human between life and death.

Three

I thought I had heard her play that song before,
as she gazed at me from the piano,
it was the light skin girl with the ethnic hair,
the one who had somehow found the means to my heart.

I thought I had heard that voice before,
singing that song as if she had awoken from an operatic
dream.

I never quite could get close to her lips,
sparkled like a shiny glass,
and almost seemed to glisten in the sunlight.

For no woman had ever captured me like that,
twisted me with those amber eyes she did,
reminded me of my younger days.

If I was the earth and she the sea,

we'd make the perfect combination,
leading to three.

Suspense I

She counted the minutes before deciding if she would make love to him once more, the one who had made her feel as if she was trapped in a dream.
It had always been about self control, but something in her made her lose control.

She might have counted the seconds too, for she lay there seated on the bed like a seated Egyptian statue,
not knowing how long things would last and if they did, would time only make it more painful.

Once, she had thought she was under control,
but love was like that, mysteriously delicious in its own right.

Suspense II

She heard the door knob turn as she began to look at her blue
eyes in the mirror,
many times she hated herself when she did.
He walked through the door of the hotel and noticed her
beautiful blond hair.

She smiled at him, looking in the mirror,
that man who had lied so many times,
she wondered,
she wondered what he had done to make her feel so good,
and so bad at the same time.

His light brown eyes melted into hers,
and they passionately danced their way to the bed,
he devoured her, and she devoured him,
and they let the physical take over.

Suspense III

She collected herself after he had left,
feeling the shame of what she had done, all that time she had
stayed away from him,
only to fall once more like a fallen angel who had gotten a
second chance.

It made her feel worse,
it made her feel worse…
that there had once been a "good guy" who had once loved
her,
and she threw that away too, the way you throw away
leftovers after dinner.

Destiny

We cannot let go of the perfectly shaped pieces it lays for us.
Though our eyes perceive imperfection, only it knows its
role.

We are caught under its own prophetic puzzle.

The human sees the fire of deception and it embraces it
foolishly
as if it causes no harm.

Destiny blinds us from the wisdom that surrounds us,
turning our senses into sheets of paper.

Though we may dream,
though we may dream,
we must admit of its power on us,
and the power we have on it,
for we are one.